San Francisco is an idy'¯
most diverse and dyna
something for everyor
scapes, and neighbour
happenings, its very vil
charmed and recharge

M000014108

CITIx60: San Francisco explores the City by the Bay in five aspects, covering architecture, art spaces, shops and markets, as well as dining and entertainment. With expert advice from 60 stars in its creative scene, this book guides you to the real attractions of the city for an authentic slice of San Francisco life.

Contents

Before You Go

BASIC INFO

Currency
US Dollar (USD / $)
Exchange rate: $1 = €0.85

Time zone
GMT −8
DST −7
DST begins at 0200 (local time) on the second Sunday in March and ends at 0200 (local time) on the first Sunday in November.

Dialling
International calling: +1
Citywide: 408, 415, 510, 650, 707, 925
Always include the area code for calls. Dial 1 for domestic calls, or 001 for calls made from outside the US.

Weather (avg. temperature range)
Spring (Mar–May): 9-17°C / 48-63°F
Summer (Jun–Aug): 11-23°C / 52-73°F
Autumn (Sep–Nov): 10-22°C / 50-70°F
Winter (Dec–Feb): 7-15°C / 45-59°F

USEFUL WEBSITES

Getting around San Francisco
www.sfmta.com

US visa application
travel.state.gov/content/travel/en/
us-visas.html

EMERGENCY CALLS

Ambulance, fire or police
911

Official visitor information centre (ViC)
+1 (415) 391 2000

Consulates
China   +1 (415) 852 5900
Japan   +1 (415) 780 6000
France   +1 (415) 397 4330
Germany   +1 (415) 775 1061
UK   +1 (415) 617 1300

AIRPORT EXPRESS TRANSFERS

SFO Airport <–> Downtown San Francisco (BART)
From International Terminal to Civic Center / Powell St. / Montgomery St. / Embarcadero:
0500-2353 (Mo-Fr), 0630– (Sa), 0800– (Su)
$9.65 one-way (free for 4–)
Trains / Journey: Every 15 mins / 30 mins

OAK Airport <–> Downtown San Francisco (BART)
From airport to Civic Center / Powell St. / Montgomery St. / Embarcadero (Coliseum Station):
0500-0000 (Mo-Fr), 0600– (Sa), 0800– (Su)
$10.95 one-way (free for 4–)
Trains / Journey: Every 6-20 mins / 45 mins

OAK Airport <–> Downtown Oakland (BART)
From airport to 12th St. / Oakland City Center (Coliseum Station):
0500-0000 (Mo-Fr), 0600– (Sa), 0800– (Su)
$8.65 one-way (free for 4–)
Trains / Journey: Every 6-20 mins / 30 mins

PUBLIC TRANSPORT

Muni* (buses, metro trains, streetcars, cable cars)
Lyft / Uber
Ford GoBike
Taxi
BART
*A single ride fare is good for 90 mins of travel

FEDERAL / PUBLIC HOLIDAYS

January	1 New Year's Day, Dr. MLK Jr. Day (3rd Mo)
February	President's Day (3rd Mo)
May	Memorial Day (Last Mo)
July	4 Independence Day
September	Labour Day (Last Mo)
October	Columbus Day (2nd Mo)
November	11 Veteran's Day, Thanksgiving (4th Th & Fr)
December	25 Christmas Day

If a federal / public holiday falls on a weekend, the next weekday becomes a 'substitute' day.

FESTIVALS / EVENTS

January
SF Sketchfest
www.sfsketchfest.com

February
San Francisco Tribal, Folk & Textile Arts Show
sanfranciscotribalandtextileartshow.com
SF IndieFest
sfindie.com
Noise Pop Music & Arts Festival
www.noisepopfest.com

April
San Francisco International Film Festival
www.sffilm.org

May
Bay to Breakers
baytobreakers.com

June
Stern Grove Festival
www.sterngrove.org
San Francisco Design Week
www.sfdesignweek.org
San Francisco Pride Parade
sfpride.org

July
SF Art Book Fair
sfartbookfair.com

September
San Francisco Fashion Week
www.sffw.fashion

October
ArtSpan Open Studios
www.artspan.org/sf-open-studios
Treasure Island Music Festival
www.treasureislandfestival.com
San Francisco Street Food Festival
sfstreetfoodfest.com

Event dates may vary by year.
Please check for updates online.

UNUSUAL OUTINGS

Emperor Norton's Fantastic Time Machine Tour
www.upout.com/sf/do/emperor-nortons-
fantastic-sf-time-machine-1

Winchester Mystery House Tour
www.winchestermysteryhouse.com

Adults-only Tenderloin Tour
www.tenderloinmuseum.org/tours

Secret Food Tour
www.secretfoodtours.com/san-francisco

San Francisco's Magic Bus Experience
magicbussf.com

SMARTPHONE APPS

Route planners
Routesy (iOS only) / MuniMobile

Curated event listings
DoStuff / SF/Arts Express

Weather forecast
Mr. Chilly (iOS only)

Area guide
NPS Golden Gate National Recreation Area

REGULAR EXPENSES

1 cup of cappuccino
$4–4.60

1 Muni ticket (one-way)
$2.75

Gratuities
F&B: 20% on bill subtotal at restaurants, bars,
food trucks
Hotels: $1–3 per bag / cab for doorman / bellhop,
$3–5 per day for cleaning service, $5–10 for
concierge
Transport & services: 15–20% on bill subtotal
for drivers, hairdressers, massage therapists,
tour guides

Count to 10

What makes San Francisco so special?

Illustrations by Guillaume Kashima aka Funny Fun

The phrase 'I left my heart in San Francisco' resonates for a reason. Although it is a popular tourist destination full of well-known attractions, countless surprises lie hidden up its colourful sleeve. As covering every facet will be impossible in a single trip, here are some quintessentially local must-sees, must-dos, and must-buys in this city teeming with unique eclecticism and energy.

WELCOME TO SAN FRANCISCO!!!

1

The Great Outdoors

Bike to the ocean
Golden Gate Park
goldengatepark.com

Hike for the famous SF fog
Marin Headlands
www.nps.gov/goga/marin-headlands.htm

Ride a ferry across the bay
SF Bay Ferry
sanfranciscobayferry.com

Sail on a schooner from 1891
SF Maritime National Historical Park
www.nps.gov/safr/index.htm

Stroll along an iconic waterfront
The Embarcadero,
Embarcadero Blvd, CA 94111

 2

 3

4

Neighbourhoods

The Mission
A lively area full of bars,
restaurants & shops

Chinatown
The largest Chinese enclave
outside of Asia

The Presidio
For history, hiking &
The Walt Disney Family Museum

North Beach
Where beat poets & writers
used to gather

Haight-Ashbury
The eclectic birthplace of
hippie counterculture

Dogpatch
A budding creative haven with
an industrial flavour

Mission Burritos

Papalote Mexican Grill
www.papalote-sf.com

Taqueria El Farolito
FB: Taqueria El Farolito

El Metate
www.elmetatesf.com

La Taqueira
FB: @LaTaqSF

La Palma Mexicatessen
www.lapalmasf.com

Taqueria El Buen Sabor
FB: @ElBuenSabor

Taqueria Cancun
*taqueria-cancun.
cafes-world.com*

Caffeine Fixes

Coffee with ice cream
Blue Bottle Coffee
bluebottlecoffee.com

Coffee with toast
Trouble Coffee
www.trouble.coffee

Irish coffee
The Buena Vista
www.thebuenavista.com

An espresso
Sightglass Coffee
sightglasscoffee.com

A latte
Artís Coffee
www.artiscoffee.com

A coffee-egg cream soda
Andytown Coffee
www.andytownsf.com

5

Leisurely Pursuits

Record digging at a legendary SF store
Amoeba Music
www.amoeba.com

Graffiti hunting
Clarion Alley (#21)

Live blues at SF's oldest bar
The Saloon
FB: @saloonsf

Live artistic performances
SF Ballet
www.sfballet.org

Golden State Warriors basketball game
Oracle Arena
www.oraclearena.com

SF Giants baseball game
AT&T Park
sanfrancisco.giants.mlb.com/
sf/ballpark

6

Baked Staples

Sourdough bread
Tartine Bakery (#40)

Whole-wheat raisin toast
The Mill (#38)

'The Rebel Within' muffin
Craftsman & Wolves
www.craftsman-wolves.com

Kouign-amann
b. patisserie
bpatisserie.com

Chocolate croissant
Arsicault
FB: Arsicault Bakery

German rye bread
Firebrand Artisan Breads
www.firebrandbread.com

The 'Cruffin'
Mr. Holmes Bakehouse
mrholmesbakehouse.com

7

Local Buys

A bud vase or mug
Heath Ceramics (#26)

A surfboard
Mollusk Surf Shop
mollusksurfshop.com

A custom bike messenger bag
Timbuk2
www.timbuk2.com

Outdoor gear
Alite
alitedesigns.com

Handmade clogs
Bryr
www.bryrstudio.com

Freshly made chocolate
Dandelion Chocolate
www.dandelionchocolate.com

A souvenir shirt
Oaklandish
www.oaklandish.com

8

Ice Cream

Popular home-grown specialty
IT's–IT
www.itsiticecream.com

Jasmine green tea flavour
Mr. & Mrs. Miscellaneous
699 22nd St, CA 94107

Organic soft serve
Twirl and Dip
www.twirlanddip.com

Orange cardamom flavour
Bi-Rite Creamery
biritecreamery.com

Seasonal flavours
Mitchell's Homemade Ice Cream
mitchellshomemade.com

Adventurous flavours
Humphry Slocombe
www.humphryslocombe.com

9

Good Reads

Obscure magazines
Issues
www.issuesshop.com/
index2.html

Used books
Walden Pond Books
www.waldenpondbooks.com

Local reads
Adobe Books
www.adobebooks.com

Free arts publication
SF Arts Quarterly
sfaq.us

World literature
City Lights Bookstore
www.citylights.com

**Extensive collection of
old & new gems**
Green Apple Books
www.greenapplebooks.com

10

Day Trips*

**Sift through antiques at
Ohmega Salvage before
dinner at Camino**
www.ohmegasalvage.com,
caminorestaurant.com

**Eat BBQ oysters at
The Marshall Store**
www.themarshallstore.com

Surf at Linda Mar
www.parks.ca.gov/?page_id=524

**Lunch at Mill Valley Beerworks
before hiking Mount Tamalpais**
www.millvalleybeerworks.com,
www.parks.ca.gov/?page_id=471

Get tipsy at Scribe Winery
scribewinery.com

Picnic at Grey Whale Cove
www.parks.ca.gov/?page_id=528

*Recommended by Aleishall Girard
Maxon & Caroline Reece

Icon Index

 Opening hours

 Address

 Contact number

 Remarks

 Admission fee

 Facebook page

 Website address

 Scan QR codes to access Google Maps and discover the area around each destination. Internet connection required.

60x60

60 Local Creatives x 60 Hotspots

From the vast and varied cityscapes to the smallest snippets of daily life, there is much to be inspired by in San Francisco. Let 60x60 point you to 60 haunts where 60 arbiters of taste whet their appetites for creative pursuits.

Landmarks & Architecture
SPOTS · 01 – 12

Besides the iconic structures and buildings that make up its urban éclat, San Francisco's natural landscapes are truly something else. Remember to pack a jacket.

Cultural & Art Spaces
SPOTS · 13 – 24

San Francisco brims with creativity and character. Quench your thirst for new ideas, whether you visit renowned galleries, local showcases, or more obscure spaces.

Markets & Shops
SPOTS · 25 – 36

With a focus on everything fresh and local, shopping in San Francisco is a meaningful affair. Be prepared to splurge on artisanal items and handcrafted goods with a Cali flair.

Restaurants & Cafés
SPOTS · 37 – 48

The San Francisco dining scene is a delicious mishmash of flavours, enhanced by high-quality local produce. Indulge in interesting concepts or gorge on fuss-free classics.

Nightlife
SPOTS · 49 – 60

There is more to fun after dark in San Francisco than hitting the bars and clubs. Change things up with tipsy bowling or a night at the museum just for adults.

Landmarks & Architecture

Inspiring iconic structures and lush natural landscapes

Even if you already have a clear picture in your mind of what to expect before you go, San Francisco in the flesh will still take you pleasantly by surprise. Besides familiar icons like the cable cars and Painted Ladies or famous attractions like the Golden Gate Bridge (#1), Alcatraz Island (www.nps.gov/alca/index.htm), Fisherman's Wharf (www.fishermanswharf.org), and Lombard Street, its verdant pockets of nature will entice you outdoors with lots of things to see and do. Go for hikes at Lands End (#2) and Twin Peaks (501 Twin Peaks Blvd, CA 94114) to unplug and unwind, or rent a bike around Golden Gate Park, where there are gardens (#9), lakes, and museums (#15, #49) to explore. If time is not of the essence, plan free-and-easy day trips to nearby places like Marin County, Point Reyes or Sonoma County for different views and vibes. More of an urbanite? Seek out one of the city's many viewpoints overlooking the skyline like Coit Tower (#5) to survey the textures that make up its rich architectural fabric. After casting your eyes across the foggy rolling hills and sparkling waters of the Pacific, or getting lost in colourful neighbourhoods with their eclectic blend of historical buildings and local character, you will leave San Francisco charmed and knowing that it is, in fact, a living and breathing masterpiece.

Palace of Fine Arts, P.020

Cass Calder Smith
Architect

A prolific architect whose award-wining work has been recognised in The New York Times, Architectural Record, Metropolis, Dwell, Interior Design, and Abitare, among others.

The Golden Gate Bridge
P.014

Lands End
P.015

Birgit Sfat
Founder, Over The Ocean

Moved from Munich to San Francisco in 2013 with her husband and daughter. Enjoys surfing, long walks with the dog, and the city's open, casual, and adventurous spirit.

Anna Chiu
Founder, KAMPERETT

Anna Chiu and Valerie Santillo design an ethical collection of womenswear focused on subtly elegant and luxurious pieces that are effortless, comfortable, and timeless.

Sutro Baths
P.016

Marcela Pardo Ariza
Visual artist & curator

A visual artist and curator from Bogota, living and working in San Francisco. Employs photography and sculpture to deal with the relationship between humour, absurdity, and representation.

Bernal Heights Hill
P.017

Coit Tower
P.018

Michal Palmer
Musician, The Bilinda Butchers

The Bilinda Butchers are a dream pop group based in San Francisco that experiments with genre-blending and dramatic themes to create sprawling, cinematic music.

Studio O+A
Interior design studio

A Cooper Hewitt Award-winning interior design firm. With their roots in workplace design, they are active members of the international arts community and strong advocates for design education.

San Francisco Art Institute
P.019

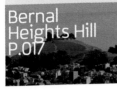

Jon Reyman
Hair stylist & entrepreneur

A leading hair stylist, business owner, educator, and collaborative partner to influential designers in the industry. Leads up to 20 Fashion Week shows.

Cathedral of St Mary of the Assumption
P.021

Future Cities Lab
Art & design studio

An experimental art and design studio, workshop, and urban think tank. Collaborator of award-winning projects exploring the intersections of art and design with advanced fabrication technologies, robotics, responsive building systems, and public spaces.

James L. Tucker
Founder, The Aesthetic Union

Printmaker and founder of The Aesthetic Union, which specialises in studio supplies and letterpress editions with artists. It also serves as his personal studio.

Palace of Fine Arts
P.020

San Francisco Botanical Garden
P.022

Brian Singer
Artist

A San Francisco–based artist who has received international attention for his provocative social initiatives such as TWIT Spotting (Texting while in Traffic) and The 1000 Journals Project.

140 Maiden Lane
P.024

Leo Jung
Art director & designer

A San Francisco–based art director, designer, and illustrator. Currently, the Creative Director of Pop-Up Magazine Productions, a media company.

Thomas Hutchings
Creative director, Landor

A creative director with over 15 years of experience in the branding and design industry. Loves harnessing the power of emotion and simple ideas to inspire and develop brands.

Mission Dolores Park
P.023

Contemporary Jewish Museum
P.025

1 The Golden Gate Bridge
Map C, P.106

Although it is one of the city's most touristy attractions and perhaps its most prominent landmark, there is much truth to all the hype. Opened in 1937, this bridge reaches 746 feet skywards and is only supported by two cables measuring >7,000 feet: deeming it one of the 7 wonders in the modern world by the American Society of Civil Engineers. To seek refuge from the perpetual crowds, rent a bike and cycle across to the beautiful town of Sausalito, or splurge on a table at one of the restaurants overlooking the structure and take it all in.

🕓 0900-1800 daily except Thanksgiving, Christmas [Welcome Centre]
🏠 Golden Gate Bridge, CA
📞 (415) 426 5220 [Welcome Centre]
🔗 goldengatebridge.org

"It's beautiful on both a sunny or foggy day – totally different experiences. Walk to the middle."

– Cass Calder Smith

2 Lands End
Map K, P.110

Whether you start by exploring points of interest like the Sutro Baths (#3) or plan for a scenic picnic at Lands End Point, this park will make for a fulfilling day outdoors. While the varying terrains along its Coastal Trail can be challenging for some due to weatherworn paths, those who press on along the windswept shoreline will look back on their experience with no regrets. Savour breathtaking vistas of the bay and the Golden Gate Bridge (#1) over majestic cliffs, speckled with shipwrecks and humpback whales in the distance if you are lucky!

🕐 0900-1700 daily (Visitors' Centre)
🏠 680 Point Lobos Ave, CA 94121
📞 (415) 426 5240 (Visitors' Centre)
🔗 www.nps.gov/goga/planyourvisit/landsend.htm

"It might get windy, so it's best to wear a jacket or hoodie."
– Birgit Sfat

3 Sutro Baths
Map K, P.110

Once the world's largest public indoor swimming pool complex that could accommodate up to 10,000 people and 1.7 million gallons of ocean water, the haunting ruins of the Sutro Baths provide visitors today with glimpses of a fading glorious past as well as some of the city's most picturesque viewpoints to take in panoramas of the Pacific. Afterwards, drop by for a meal at the nearby Cliff House, another iconic piece of architectural history formerly owned by Adolph Sutro, the German-born entrepreneur who helped to shape San Francisco's landscape in the late 19th century.

🕑 0900–1700 daily [Visitors' Centre]
🏠 Point Lobos Ave, CA 94121
📞 (415) 426–5240 [Visitors' Centre]
🌐 www.sutrobaths.com

"Go during sunset; it's the most beautiful view."

– Anna Chiu, KAMPERETT

4 Bernal Heights Hill
Map L, P.110

Located to the south of the bustling hive of activity that is the Mission district, Bernal Heights Hill is a welcome breath of fresh air with its slow charm. Seasoned hikers and beginners alike will enjoy the short stroll up to the top, where sweeping views stretch as far as the eye can see. Along the way, try to spot kestrels, alligator lizards, or other species from the diverse wildlife that call this hill home. As it is also a dog-friendly park, you might stumble upon some of the neighbourhood's furry residents doing the same!

🕐 0500-0000 daily
🏠 Bernal Heights Blvd, CA 94110
🔗 sfrecpark.org/destination/
bernal-heights-park

"The hike to the top is short and always worth it."

– Marcela Pardo Ariza

5 **Coit Tower**
Map G, P.108

Named after the wealthy eccentric who left
behind a substantial bequest to beautify her
beloved city upon her death, Coit Tower has
been an integral part of San Francisco's skyline
since it was completed in 1933. Standing at
210 feet tall amid the renowned habitat of
wild parrots that is Telegraph Hill, this art deco
monument was built in part as a memorial
to its benefactor and houses beautiful fresco
murals that depict life during the Great Depres-
sion. Pay a small price to take the elevator up
to the observation deck and be rewarded with
unobstructed 360-degree cityscapes.

🕙 1000-1800 (May-Oct), -1700 (Nov-Apr)
🏠 1 Telegraph Hill Blvd, CA 94133
📞 (415) 249 0995 🔳 sfrecpark.org/destination/
telegraph-hill-pioneer-park/coit-tower
🎫 Observation Deck: $8/$5/$2/Free for 4-

"Take the back way via the Filbert Steps. Once you're
at Coit Tower, head back down towards North Beach
for some great pizza."

– Michal Palmer, The Bilinda Butchers

6 San Francisco Art Institute

Map F, P.108

As one of the oldest and most reputable art schools in the country, the San Francisco Art Institute (SFAI) is more than just a place of higher learning. Founded as the San Francisco Art Association in 1871 by influential members of the creative community, its illustrious alumni have continued to shake the art world ever since. Those who are tired of morose museums will find its galleries refreshing, such as the one featuring a specially commissioned mural by its legendary namesake, Diego Rivera. After enjoying the exhibitions, stop by the rooftop café for a snack and stellar city views.

🕐 0830–2000 (Mo–Th), –1500 (Fr) [SFAI Café]
🏠 800 Chestnut St, CA 94133
📞 (415) 771 7020
🔗 www.sfai.edu

"[SFAI] combines periods of classic and modernist architecture in an abrupt way. It works even though the 'changes' are sudden."

– Studio O+A

019

7 Palace of Fine Arts
Map C, P.107

At first glance, the Palace of Fine Arts looks like a backdrop in a movie set with its rosy rococo façade and classical Roman-inspired architecture. Originally built for the 1915 Panama-Pacific Exposition to exhibit works of art, it currently plays host to a variety of live performances from all over the world in its indoor theatre. Although the monumental structure has been rebuilt and renovated over the years, it still retains its quiet grandeur. The beautiful park is free to explore, so go for a picnic and pose for pictures by the swan lagoon, or catch the sunset and stay on for a tranquil night stroll.

🕐 1000-1700 (Tu-Su)
🏠 3601 Lyon St, CA 94123
📞 (415) 608 2220
URL palaceoffinearts.com

"*A beautiful place for a picnic or a stroll to admire the stunning architecture. Dress warmly; it gets windy.*"

– Jon Reyman

8 Cathedral of Saint Mary of the Assumption

Map A, P.102

Otherwise known as Saint Mary's Cathedral, this distinct landmark's brutalist architecture celebrates artistic and engineering brilliance, while showcasing a fascinating fusion of modern sensibilities and religious iconography. While its clever use of lines and lighting for dramatic effect is internationally renowned, the church is also famous amongst locals for the scandalous shadow that it casts outside at a certain time of the day; thought to resemble the silhouette of a shapely woman's breast. Plan your visit around a sunny afternoon.

🕐 0730-1700 (Mo-Fr & Su), 0800- (Sa) for viewing
🏠 1111 Gough St, CA 94109
📞 (415) 567 2020
🌐 stmarycathedralsf.org

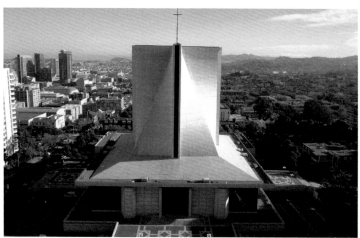

"As long as you don't intrude on mass, you'll be able to walk in and see the breathtaking ceiling structure."

– Future Cities Lab

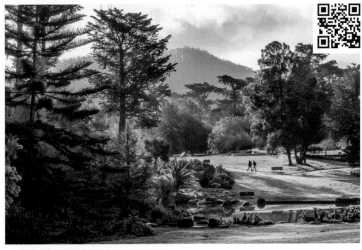

9 **San Francisco Botanical Garden**
Map H, P.109

Weary spirits will find respite and rejuvenation in this botanical wonderland filled with more than 8,500 varieties of plants from all over the world. Have a wander through sprawling open spaces and immaculately landscaped gardens where flower collections change every season. From lectures to special tours, the opportunities to reflect on the mysteries of life are endless. Families with kids can picnic, listen to stories, or hunt for bugs as part of the Youth Education programme.

🕐 *0730–1600/–1700/–1800 daily, depending on season* 💲 *$8/$5/$2/Free for 4–* 🏠 *1199 9th Ave, CA 94122* 🌐 *www.sfbotanicalgarden.org* 🔗 *Free entry on Thanksgiving, Christmas, NY, 2nd Tu monthly, & 0730–0900 daily*

"If you're lucky, you might stumble across an art piece happening, a symphony playing, or a full moon walk. Check out their calendar for details."
– James L. Tucker

10 Mission Dolores Park
Map B, P.104

Having spurred creative and liberal movements across generations since the Gold Rush, San Francisco's carefree spirit is an irresistible force that continues to define and distinguish her people. Soak up some authentic local vibes by veering away from a packed sightseeing itinerary to simply hang out at this lush 14-acre park. It is the perfect place to laze on a patch of lawn or under a shady palm tree to people watch, as you never know what interesting characters might turn up! Be sure to pick up after yourself when leaving this 'leave no trace' public space.

🕙 0600-2200 daily
📍 19th & Dolores St, CA 94114
🔗 sfrecpark.org/destination/mission-dolores-park

HELEN DILLER PLAYGROUND
AT MISSION DOLORES PARK

"Walk to the top, sit on a bench, and look at the view. Depending on the time of year, there are also outdoor movie nights and other activities."
– Brian Singer

11 140 Maiden Lane
Map A, P.102

Known for organically blending his structures into their surroundings to showcase natural beauty, Frank Lloyd Wright designed this simple yet striking building for the V. C. Morris Gift Shop in 1948. While its bricked façade is easy to miss, discerning eyes will notice its subtle changes in appearance depending on where light hits. Even though different tenants have occupied the space over the years, ask inside to take a closer look at the undulating walkway that many believe was the physical prototype of his iconoclastic masterpiece in New York.

🕐 1000–1800 (Mo–Sa), 1200–1700 (Su)
🏠 140 Maiden Ln, CA 94108
📞 (415) 500 4930
URL *www.isaia.it*

"The unmistakable winding staircase was a proof of concept for the circular ramp that characterises the Guggenheim."

– Leo Jung

12 Contemporary Jewish Museum

Map A, P.102

Piercing the San Francisco skyline since opening in 2008, this museum's soaring blue steel structure is an architectural marvel with a purposeful juxtaposition. Although it was constructed using futuristic materials and cutting-edge technique, its raison d'être is still deeply rooted in religious meaning. Originally built as a power station in 1881, it owes its unusual exterior to Hebrew letters that spell 'life' when put together. Besides its unexpectedly sleek interior design, the dynamic displays and themed exhibitions throughout the year also make it worth stepping inside for.

🕐 1100-1700 (Fr-Tu), -2000 (Th)
💲 $14/$12/$5/Free for 18-
🏠 736 Mission St, CA 94103
URL www.thecjm.org
🎟 Free entry 1st Tu monthly

"Tropisueno is a great place to eat nearby."

– Thomas Hutchings

Cultural & Art Spaces

Colourful enclaves and world-renowned museums

Many cities profess to be a vibrant melting pot of cultures, but there is something about San Francisco that makes it especially magnetic. Having been the hub of liberal activism since the Gold Rush and the birthplace of United Nations in 1945, its 'anything is possible' ethos easily rivals New York's and continues to attract kindred spirits from all over the world. Even as the revolutionary hippie and peace movements in the past have paved the way for today's innovative start-ups shaking up the tech scene, it is still the place to be seen and heard. Bask in its palpable creative energy at world-renowned art spaces like SFMOMA (#14) and the de Young Museum (#15), or smaller but no-less-significant shows around the city that celebrate all forms of expression and aspiring home-grown talents. With so many events and festivals happening, you are bound to feel a connection, whatever your interests may be. For genuine glimpses into the local way of life, simply explore the different neighbourhoods by foot to let their stories and possibilities reveal themselves to you. There is more to the city than just the biggest Chinatown outside of Asia! If you try hard enough, you can almost hear echoes from the psychedelic Summer of Love at Haight-Ashbury, or make out the faint silhouette of a Beat poet crafting his next verse in a North Beach dive bar.

Kerem Suer
Designer

A multi-disciplinary designer and a former sailor living in San Francisco. Helps tech companies design software products and takes tens of thousands of photographs of San Francisco and the Bay Area.

SFMOMA
P.031

Greg Lutze
Co-founder, VSCO

Co-founder and Chief Creative Officer of VSCO, a community for expression. VSCO has been named Apple's 'App of the Year' and one of Google Play's 'Best Apps of 2015', among others.

Travis Collinson
Visual artist

A visual artist working with the subtleties of observation, perception, and interpretation. Featured in numerous group and solo exhibitions throughout the country.

Fort Mason
Center for
Arts & Culture
P.030

de Young
Museum
P.034

Monica Garwood
Illustrator & graphic designer

An illustrator and graphic designer living and working in San Francisco. Grew up in the Bay Area and loves all it has to offer. Spends most of her time painting and playing with her dog.

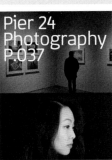

Pier 24
Photography
P.037

June Kim
Photographer

A photographer whose work and favourite locations in San Francisco reflect her love for architecture and quiet beauty.

Math Times Joy
Design studio

A husband-and-wife-led design studio based in San Francisco. Focuses on visual identity and communication design for a wide range of small businesses, entrepreneurs, and forward-thinking individuals to help build simple, expressive brands.

Spoke Art
P.036

Minnesota
Street
Project
P.038

Jameson Alexander
Founder, Park Life Store & Gallery

An art collector and design enthusiast that started Park Life Store and Gallery and Publishing Company. Originally from Southern California, but has lived in San Francisco for over 20 years.

Lydia Nichols
Illustrator & designer

An illustrator and designer with a penchant for drawing anthropomorphic animals and objects. When not doodling up a storm, she is hiking across the Bay Area and soaking up the nature.

Garrett Miller
Illustrator

A farm kid from Maryland making it in the big city. Spends much of his free time running, drawing, and harassing his cat.

David Baker
Architect

An architect and urbanist living and working in San Francisco. His firm David Baker Architects specialises in affordable and sustainable multi-family and mixed-use housing.

Carissa Potter
Founder, People I've Loved

An illustrator based in Oakland whose prints and small-scale objects reflect her hopeless romanticism through their investigations into public and private intimacy. A founding member of Colpa Press and founder of People I've Loved.

Ryan Putnam
Designer & illustrator

A designer, illustrator, potter, and father, whose approach to work is fun, personal, and always forward-looking. His goal is to combine craft, functionality with fine art integrity and the exacting principles of design.

13 Fort Mason Center for Arts & Culture

Map F, P.108

From theatre and dance performances to art installations and cultural classes, the Fort Mason Center for Arts & Culture runs an assortment of programmes to promote the arts within the community. While your day away at the galleries or tuck into a meal at the Michelin-recommended Greens Restaurant, before catching a show that you can buy tickets to online. With beautiful views of the bay as a backdrop, its outdoor events like Off The Grid – the country's largest food truck gathering – are also not to be missed.

🕐 Hours vary with events
🏠 2 Marina Blvd, Landmark Building C, Suite 260, CA 94123
📞 (415) 345 7575   URL fortmason.org

"If you're visiting between March and October, there's a food truck party every Friday with live music and food trucks from all around the city."

– Kerem Suer

14 SFMOMA
Map A, P.103

As one of the largest museums of modern and contemporary art in the world, SFMOMA is a must-visit for fans and casual browsers alike. Plan ahead by downloading the free mobile app or prepare to lose all sense of time by letting curiosity be your guide beyond its uniquely sculptured façade, where 7 floors of extraordinary works ranging from the classic to the unconventional await exploration. Need a breather between galleries? 45,000 sq ft of public spaces invite you to rest and reset, while the verdant 15,000-plant vertical garden on the third floor terrace is a sight for sore eyes.

🕙 1000-1700 (Fr-Tu), -2100 (Th) except Thanksgiving, Christmas 💲 $25/$22/$19/ Free for 18- 🏠 151 Third St, CA 94103
📞 (415) 357 4000 🔗 www.sfmoma.org

"Wear your favourite sneakers. It's a big museum so prepare to bombard your senses and plan on getting a coffee about halfway through."

– Travis Collinson

EXIT

15 de Young Museum
Map H, P.109

Designed by the Swiss firm Herzog & de Meuron of London's Tate Modern fame, the de Young Museum is a multifaceted destination that integrates brilliant architecture, the natural landscape, and beautiful art in the form of special themed exhibits and permanent collections from all over the world. After roaming around the thoroughly immersive galleries, amble along to the nearby Japanese Tea Garden to reflect on all that you have just seen, or browse the two-story museum store for art books, distinctive decorative objects, and educational toys as gifts or souvenirs.

🕙 0930-1715 (Tu-Su)
💲 $15/$10/$6/Free for 17-
🏠 50 Hagiwara Tea Garden Dr, CA 94118
📞 (415) 750 3600
🌐 deyoung.famsf.org

"No visit is complete without exploring the Hamon Observation Tower, a glass-enclosed area allowing breathtaking views of San Francisco and the Bay."

– Greg Lutze

16 Spoke Art
Map A, P.102

Not many art galleries attract cosplaying fans on opening nights, and for this, Spoke Art stands out from its peers. With an emphasis on accessibility, its themed exhibitions centre around pop culture and tributes to movies, directors, and TV shows – ensuring that almost anybody can appreciate the creativity on display. Check out the changing monthly exhibits and have a chuckle at familiar subject matter expressed with a twist through paintings, sculptures, and illustrations. Looking for a fun memento? Get an alternative film poster or original prints by the local talents featured.

🕐 1000–1800 (Tu-Sa)
🏠 816 Sutter St, CA 94109
☎ (415) 796-3774
URL spoke-art.com

"Next door, there's another great gallery space called Hashimoto Contemporary."
– Monica Garwood

17 Pier 24 Photography
Map A, P.103

If there ever were an ultimate pilgrimage that photographers or photography enthusiasts had to make, it would be to Pier 24 Photography. As the largest space in the world dedicated solely to art in this medium, visitors can count on an impressive curation of works ranging from the iconic to the underrated – all of which they can enjoy in quiet contemplation within a cavernous warehouse setting. As there are usually no labels accompanying the pieces, ask for a gallery guidebook before your tour or get help from a friendly docent nearby.

🕐 0900–1715 (Mo–Fr) by appointment only
💲 Price varies with shows
🏠 Pier 24, The Embarcadero, CA 94105
☎ (415) 512 7424 URL pier24.org

"Go online early to snag a reservation – it's worth it."
– June Kim

18 Minnesota Street Project
Map B, P.105

Founded to provide affordable and sustainable spaces for artists, galleries, and related non-profit organisations, the Minnesota Street Project is a lifeline for the local creative community. Spanning across three warehouses, it offers visitors a visual journey into the city's future of art. After an inspiring afternoon of gallery viewing, round off your trip by grabbing a bite at one of the many culinary hotspots that have been sprouting around the Dogpatch district.

🕑 *Hours vary with galleries*
🏠 1275 Minnesota St, CA 94107
📞 (415) 243 0825
URL www.minnesotastreetproject.com

"Before or after, grab a bite to eat or coffee at Piccino's, or dessert at Mr. & Mrs. Miscellaneous (their housemade peanut butter malt balls are a must)!"
– Math Times Joy

19 Creative Growth
Map N, P.111

Embodying San Francisco's 'can-do' ethos is Creative Growth, a non-profit organisation for artists with developmental, mental, and physical disabilities. It runs a vibrant studio programme where they can express themselves through various mediums, develop their skills with classes, and be represented for shows all around the world. Day-trippers to Oakland can pop by this inspiring space, where paintings, ceramics, and sculptures are exhibited and available for purchase. For lunch or dinner, hunt for Homeroom Mac & Cheese (#48) to discover new twists on a familiar favourite.

🕐 1000–1630 (Mo–Fr), –1500 (Sa)
🏠 55 24th St, Oakland, CA 94612
📞 (510) 836 0769
🔗 www.creativegrowth.org

"Take a tour of the art studios or buy something from their gallery or store."
– Jameson Alexander

20 826 Valencia / Pirate Supply Store

Map B, P.104

826 Valencia is a non-profit organisation that helps under-resourced students with their creative writing skills. Set up by local literary hero Dave Eggers, it is funded through themed retail fronts that sell products created by volunteer artists and designers. At the Pirate Supply Store, related treasures and tongue-in-cheek paraphernalia are stuffed into every nook and cranny of the shop interior, fashioned after the belly of a ship. Proceeds from your purchase help aspiring talents, so you will be 'looting' for a good cause.

🕐 1200–1800 daily
🏠 826 Valencia St, CA 94110
📞 (415) 642 5905, ext: 201
🔗 826valencia.org/store

"Be sure to check out 826's other – and differently themed – stores in DC, LA, Chicago, NYC, Boston, and Michigan."

– Lydia Nichols

21 Clarion Alley

Map B, P.104

In a city teeming with artistic endeavours, it comes as no surprise that San Francisco embraces the authenticity and beauty of street art as a voice for the community and a vehicle of collaboration. The Clarion Alley Mural Project was established to place culture and dignity over profit and the rules of private property. Since it began in 1992, this Mission district block has been used as a canvas by artists of all ethnicities, ages, and styles. Besides admiring the talent on display or finding colourful backdrops for your photos, take in the meaningful messages behind each mural and come away enlightened.

🏠 Off Valencia St btw 17th & 18th St, CA 94110
🔗 clarionalleymuralproject.org

"*Walk through the alleyway and then get ramen at Ken Ken Ramen (#44) around the corner. Wander to Dolores Park (#10) after and soak in some rays.*"

– Garrett Miller

22 StoreFrontLab
Map B, P.104

Art is all about breaking boundaries, and in the case of StoreFrontLab, they refer to the ones between performer and audience. Set up to prompt thought-provoking dialogue and public discourse, its repertoire ranges from interactive installations, participatory projects, and artistic experiments to lectures and workshops that revolve around the community, creativity, and local industry. Go with an open mind and let your voice be heard during a riveting discussion, or if you hate being dragged into the spotlight, check online for an indie film screening, poetry reading session, or live gig.

🕐 Hours vary with events
🏠 337 Shotwell St, CA 94110
📞 (415) 845 0646
URL www.storefrontlab.org

"*Events are free but you should register for them. And, be prepared to participate!*"

– David Baker

 23 500 Capp Street
Map B, P.104

As an artist whose work revolved around finding the beauty in everyday things and making art a part of daily life, David Ireland's 1886 Italianate-style home encapsulates his philosophies flawlessly, both as a vessel for his creations and as a masterpiece in itself. Besides being able to examine his sculptures and assemblages more closely, visitors will get an intimate glimpse into how he might have lived, making it a uniquely personal experience. Look out for temporary exhibitions by other artists, staged in different parts of the house throughout the year.

🕓 1100, 1400, 1600 (Mo-We) for guided tours; 1200-1700 (Sa) 🏠 500 Capp St, CA 94110
📞 +33 (0)1 4069 9600
🔗 500cappstreet.org

"Book tickets in advance."
– Carissa Potter

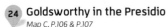

24 Goldsworthy in the Presidio
Map C, P.106 & P.107

See art in a whole new light through Goldsworthy in the Presidio, an organically evolving project by Andy Goldsworthy that is nestled within the forest park. Famous for working with materials such as twigs, leaves, and snow for his natural masterpieces, the British artist and environmentalist used trees felled as part of reforestation efforts to create his site-specific installations – Spire (2008) and Wood Line (2011) – with each one articulating a different meaning grounded in its surroundings. Take the three-mile hike for a unique way to connect with creativity and nature.

🕐 *Daily [Spire/Wood Line], 1000–1600 (Sa, Su) or by appointment [Tree Fall]* 🏠 *Locations vary around the Presidio district* 📞 *(415) 362 9330/(415) 561 2767 for appointment* 🔗 *www.for-site.org/project/goldsworthy-in-the-presidio*

"Visit the installations at different parts of the day. You can have different experiences depending on the the sun, temperature, and surroundings."

– Ryan Putnam

JUICE
CRACKERS
CHOCOLATE

VEGGIE
CHIPS
DRIED
FRUIT

OUR PICK
OF THE WEEK
FRANCHISE
MAGAZINE

Markets & Shops

Fresh and artisanal items with distinctive Californian touches

Shopping in San Francisco is a risky affair, in that it can leave the incautious traveller with a much lighter wallet! If you enjoy window-shopping and whiling the day away at the mall, Union Square (unionsquareshop.com) is a 2.4-acre public plaza and historical landmark filled with big chains, flagship stores, restaurants, beauty salons, and theatres for your browsing pleasure. Side streets around the area are also worth the wander, where you could stumble across some hidden retail gems. For truly worthwhile splurges, skip the run-of-the-mill brands and seek out the wide variety of independent shops around the city featuring quirky finds, vintage treasures, and quintessential designs oozing with California cool like Tail of the Yak (#31), Paxton Gate (#34), and General Store (shop-generalstore.com). As a creative hub, San Francisco is not just about cutting-edge style or off-the-runway trends. It celebrates local artisans who take pride in their goods and craftsmanship, so expect not to leave empty-handed from places like Heath Ceramics (#26) and Dandelion Chocolate (www.dandelionchocolate.com) – both within the vicinity of one of the best farmers markets in the world (#32). Plenty of opportunities will also exist for flea market enthusiasts to hunt for bargains and treasures. At the end of your trip, your best find would be a new sense of appreciation for all things carefully and wonderfully made.

James Trump
Creative director

A Creative Director at Moving Brands, an independent global creative company, and co-founder of Fells Andes, a luxury textile brand. Born and educated in the UK.

Heath
Ceramics
P.054

Caroline Reece
Co-founder, Artworklove

A French designer, art director and photographer currently working at Manual, a branding and design studio located in the Dogpatch district. Co-founded the design studio Artworklove.

Casey Gray
Artist

A full-time artist working primarily with aerosol paints and masking techniques. Born and raised in the Bay Area. Living and showing his work in San Francisco since 2008.

Song Tea
P.052

Park Life
P.056

Erik Marinovich
Co-founder, Friends of Type

A San Francisco-based lettering artist and designer who co-founded Friends of Type. In 2012, he co-founded Title Case, a creative workspace that conducts workshops and lectures.

Gravel &
Gold
P.059

David Brenner
Founder, Habitat Horticulture

A designer and creator of vertical gardens. Founded Habitat Horticulture to bring greenery into the minds and lives of city dwellers. Enjoys hiking Mt. Tam, eating pastry, and writing music.

Jayde Fish
Designer & illustrator

A San Francisco-based designer and illustrator who takes inspiration from fashion, textiles, nature, and vintage children's books. Her work has been featured in Gucci's SS2017 runway show and numerous editorials including Elle, Vogue, and Vanity Fair.

The
Aesthetic
Union
P.058

Ver Unica
P.060

Aleishall Girard Maxon
Fibre & graphic artist

Fibre and graphic artist working as the Co-creative Director of Girard Studio. Inspired by colour, texture, and the layers of both that exist in the world.

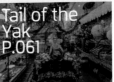

Tail of the Yak
P.061

Ferry Building Marketplace
P.062

Ann Yu
Musician, Silver Swans

Songwriter and one-half of electronic band Silver Swans. Enjoying every moment in San Francisco with her husband Seamus in a constant quest to be inspired and create.

Character San Francisco
Branding & design agency

A San Francisco-based branding and design agency with a passion for launching, rejuvenating, and propelling brands. Creates lasting and meaningful relationships through smart thinking and thoughtful design.

Flora Grubb Gardens
P.064

Nicolas Rader
Director

Director of Snøhetta's West Coast office. Currently overseeing projects such as the One Oak Tower and Plaza in San Francisco, the James Beard Public Market in Portland, and the French Laundry Kitchen Renovation and Garden Expansion.

Paxton Gate
P.065

Vinyl Dreams
P.066

Stan Zienka
Graphic designer

A graphic designer and occasional painter who has lived in San Francisco since 1999. Enjoys the majority of his time in the Mission, Dogpatch, and Bernal districts with his wife and daughter.

Brandon Jew
Chef-owner, Mister Jiu's

A San Francisco native and the chef-owner of Mister Jiu's, a Chinese-American restaurant in Chinatown. Lives in the Inner Richmond district with his wife and pup.

Bi-Rite Market
P.067

25 Song Tea
Map E, P.107

San Francisco may not be the first place that pops into mind when it comes to tea, but owner Peter Luong's love for simplicity, character, and exceptional quality permeates the store's ambience and range of products carried. Tea aficionados will enjoy taking their picks from traditional, rare, and experimental leaves originating from China and Taiwan, while homeware collectors and casual walk-ins will appreciate the gorgeous collection of masterfully crafted ceramics that seamlessly blend form and function. Join in a communal tasting session for a more intimate experience.

🕐 1100–1800 (Tu-Sa), –1700 (Su)
🏠 2120 Sutter St, CA 94115
📞 (415) 885 2118
🌐 songtea.com
✒ Tastings are on a first-come, first-served basis @ $10/pax

"Start a conversation with the staff and allow them to walk you through the intricacies of a proper tea ritual and experience."

– James Trump

26 Heath Ceramics
Map B, P.104

A shopping trip in San Francisco will not be complete without a visit to this inspiring retail space filled with design-driven goods for the table and home. Originally founded in Sausalito, Heath Ceramics is a home-grown brand that has left an indelible mark on the local creative scene by winning a slew of prestigious design awards since 1948. Prepare to splurge on some one-of-a-kind souvenirs, as it is known for its quintessential handcrafted dinnerware with a distinctly Californian aesthetic. Reservations are recommended for tours of the adjacent tile factory and showroom.

🕐 1000-1800 (Su-We), -1900 (Th-Sa)
🏠 2900 18th St, CA 94110
📞 (415) 361 5552, ext. 13
URL www.heathceramics.com
🔗 Factory Tours: 1st & 3rd Fr (1400) monthly, every Sa & Su (1130)

"If you can bear the queues, get breakfast or lunch at Tartine Manufactory (#40) in the same space."

– Caroline Reece

27 Park Life
Map D, P.107

A 1,400-sq ft independent retail store with an art gallery at the back, Park Life immerses shoppers in all things creative and cleverly designed. Stocked with fun and unique items from all over the world, you can find anything from playful Scandinavian homeware to rare out-of-print books within a diverse price range. The gallery's 10 yearly exhibits showcase some of the most engaging contemporary pieces in the art world today, while limited edition artist collaborations such as skate decks and tees make for special gifts.

🕐 1100-2000 (Mo-Sa), -1800 (Su)
🏠 220 Clement St, CA 94118
📞 (415) 386 7275
URL www.parklifestore.com

"It's slightly off the beaten track for tourists, but the neighbourhood is full of great restaurants and interesting shops."
– Casey Gray

057

28 The Aesthetic Union
Map B, P.104

The Aesthetic Union is a haven for appreciators of great design, handcraftsmanship, and
timeless approaches. Besides offering person-
alised letterpress, silkscreen, lino block, and
mimeograph printing services, it also stocks
limited edition cards, prints, notebooks, and
posters, alongside art tools and office supplies.
Join a workshop or tour of the studio for an opportunity to see how the vintage presses work
and print a one-of-a-kind souvenir. Afterwards,
freshen up with a cuppa at Blue Bottle Coffee
in the same building.

1100–1800 (Tu–Fr), –1700 (Sa, Su)
555 Alabama St, CA 94110
(732) 822 4693
www.theaestheticunion.com

"Ask for James (the owner) to give you
a tour of the shop."

– Erik Marinovich

29 Gravel & Gold

Map B, P.104

A boutique that captures the beauty of every-day moments, Gravel & Gold offers surprising finds with every visit – from cushion covers and sweaters with cheeky boob motifs to hand-embroidered statement earrings. Set up by women to support women as well as the local artist community to create apparel, accessories, homeware, and other useful everyday items that bring joy, the store also hosts art openings and design workshops. Keep an eye out for the delightful in-house collection by the ladies who run and work at the store.

🕐 1200-1900 (Mo-Sa), -1700 (Su)
🏠 3266 21st St, CA 94110
📞 (415) 552 0112
🌐 www.gravelandgold.com

"Try out their amazing hanging hammock chair!"

– David Brenner

30 Ver Unica

Map A, P.102

Vintage and second-hand clothing and accessories may not be the usual way for many to fill a wardrobe, but the impeccably-curated selection of high-quality basic and upscale picks at Ver Unica might well change a skeptical mind. As one of the favourite haunts of fashion insiders since it opened more than 20 years ago, this charming boutique remains an excellent place to find one-off gems and investment pieces to this day. Rare Levi's denim? Check. Classic 1980s Gucci? Check. The only catch? Pray that you find them in the right size!

🕐 1100–1900 (Mo–Sa), 1200–1800 (Su)
🏠 526 Hayes St, CA 94102
📞 (415) 621 6259
URL www.etsy.com/shop/VerUnicaSF

"Make sure to check out her selection of jewellery; she has a great selection of vintage and local designers."

– Jayde Fish

31 Tail of the Yak

Map P, P.111

Even if you walk through the unassuming
entrance with nothing to buy in mind, Tail of
the Yak's magical interior may persuade you
otherwise. The store's carefully selected, often
one-of-a-kind merchandise from all around
the world is always exquisitely presented, and
covers a variety of interests. Whether you
are into fabrics from France, wooden stamps
from India, silver Mexican dinnerware, antique
toys, taxidermy animals or interesting soaps
and perfumes, there is something special for
everyone. Stop by on a day trip to Berkeley.

🕐 1100–1730 (Mo–Sa)
🏠 2632 Ashby Ave, Berkeley,
CA 94705
📞 (510) 841 9891
f @TailOfTheYak

*"Plan to have some time to look around in detail.
While it is not large in size, this unique space is
overflowing with treasures large and small."*

– Aleishall Girard Maxon

32 Ferry Building Marketplace
Map G, P.108

If you are looking for some of the most incredible meal experiences that San Francisco has to offer, the Ferry Building Marketplace is the place to be. Widely acclaimed even by natives for the quality and diversity of its fresh farm produce, regional artisan specialties, and pop-up food stands by some of the city's most popular restaurants, its weekend Farmers Market is a feast for the senses. Even during the week, there are plenty of reasons to drop by, whether it is to dine on delicious local fare or hunt for souvenirs by home-grown brands.

🕐 1000-1900 (Mo-Fr), 0800-1800 (Sa), 1100-1700 (Su)
🏠 One Ferry Building, CA 94111
📞 (415) 983-8030
🔗 www.ferrybuildingmarketplace.com
🖉 Farmers Market: Tu & Th (1000-1400), Sa (0800-)

"Saturday is the best time to go, when all the vendors are out and they've set up the market near the water."

– Ann Yu, Silver Swans

33 Flora Grubb Gardens
Map M, P.111

While you are unlikely to run out of amazing café options in San Francisco, coffee at Flora Grubb Garden is an unforgettable experience. Since opening, this garden store and workshop space has been a mecca of sorts for green-thumbed city folks, with an ever-changing store façade, flourishing plant displays, and a wide variety of succulents for sale. Get your hands dirty at the Potting Bench where you can create and design your own arrangements, or simply enjoy a caffeine-fueled time-out amidst a calming, lush oasis.

🕐 0900–1700 (Mo–Sa), 1000– (Su)
🏠 1634 Jerrold Ave, CA 94124
📞 (415) 648 2670
URL www.floragrubb.com

"Visit Flora Grubb to sip coffee in their garden and enjoy the little oasis in the middle of industrial San Francisco."

– Character San Francisco

34 Paxton Gate
Map B, P.104

Stepping into Paxton Gate is akin to entering a living cave full of curios inspired by the garden and natural sciences. Its taxidermy section is especially weird and wonderful, where you can buy anything from ethically sourced fossils and animal bones to a stuffed giraffe's head - if you are allowed to bring them home! Whether you avidly collect oddities or are simply fascinated by eye-catching ephemera, every corner of this store is worth getting lost in. The Curiosities for Kids section is also an imaginative child's (and child-at-heart's) dream come true.

🕐 1100-1900 (Su-We), -2000 (Th-Sa)
🏠 824 Valencia St, CA 94110
📞 (415) 824 1872
URL paxtongate.com/index

"Go with an open mind and be ready to explore!"
– Nicolas Rader

35 Vinyl Dreams
Map I, P.109

San Francisco may be full of independent record stores for beat enthusiasts, but Vinyl Dreams is the true dance music lover's mecca when it comes to 12"s and LPs of the genre. With an exciting catalogue curated by seasoned buyer and Amoeba Music-alumnus Michelangelo Battaglia, crate diggers and serious collectors will be rewarded with forgotten favourites, rare classics, and obscure underground releases in addition to the latest hits. If you are new to collecting, park yourself at a sound station to browse or go with recommendations from the knowledgeable staff.

🕐 1400–2000 (Mo), 1300– (Tu–Sa), –1900 (Su)
🏠 593 Haight St, CA 94117
📞 (415) 379 0974
📘 @vinyldreamssf

"Check their Facebook page to find out about special in-store performances."

– Stan Zienka

36 Bi-Rite Market
Map B, P.104

The local community spirit is truly thriving at Bi-Rite Market, where meaningful relationships form the root of the business. Besides carrying a variety of fresh and artisanal products that celebrate craft, heritage, and diversity, the honest and delicious food prepared by the kitchen is akin to a warm embrace for first-time visitors craving authentic flavours. The organic ice cream by Bi-Rite Creamery is a must-have: available in original seasonal flavours and made by hand in small batches daily.

🕐 0800–2100 daily
🏠 3639 18th St, CA 94110
📞 (415) 241 9760
URL www.biritemarket.com

"Stock up here to make a meal for yourself or to get a bunch of really good snacks."

– Brandon Jew

Restaurants & Cafés

Modern dining concepts and mouthwatering comfort food

To say that San Francisco is a true food lover's paradise is hardly an overstatement. With the influx of diverse cultures since the Gold Rush, the city is akin to a mega-buffet of authentic cuisines and exciting fusions from all around the world. The constant push for creativity and a preference for fresh seasonal produce underlie the success of most kitchens in the scene, resulting in an artful elevation of familiar flavours to epicurean creations that tantalise you with a taste of the future. Places like Mister Jiu's (misterjius. com) and 'aina (#43) serve up traditional fare with a twist, while Outerlands (#39) and Lazy Bear (#42) exemplify how sublime simplicity and sincerity can be when cooking for the community takes centre stage. If you are not much of a white-tablecloth gourmand, tuck into a wide variety of comfort food and everyday staples around the city. A must-have is the Mission burrito: a tasty piece of the country's culinary history. Coffee and pastry lovers can rejoice in the numerous local options available, from brewers like Blue Bottle Coffee (bluebottlecoffee.com) and Four Barrel Coffee (#37) as well as artisan bakeries like b.patisserie (bpatisserie.com) and Tartine Manufactory (#40). To complete your trip, indulge in some seafood straight from the Pacific at Hog Island Oyster Co. (hogislandoysters.com) or Swan Oyster Depot (swanoysterdepot.us).

Kevin Tudball
Illustrator & graphic designer

An illustrator, graphic designer, and musician working as the Art Director for Four Barrel Coffee. Spends his time drawing quirky cartoons and his money on delicious food.

Four Barrel Coffee
P.072

The Mill
P.074

Casey Martin
Designer & art director

A Chicago-trained designer and art director who lives and works in San Francisco. Runs a branding and design studio in the Western Addition.

Jenny Gheith
Assistant curator

Assistant curator of painting and sculpture at SFMOMA. Commissions new work from living artists, while researching, writing, and organising exhibitions about contemporary art.

Outerlands
P.075

Tung Chiang
Director, Heath Clay Studio

A designer and ceramist who is also the Director of Heath Clay Studio. His career has been an evolution from 2D to 3D, toward a fusion of thinking, designing and making.

Tartine Manufactory
P.076

20th Century Cafe
P.077

Natalie So
Writer & editor

Writer, editor, and story producer for Epic Magazine. Publishes long-form journalism that is then developed into movies and TV shows. Born and raised in the Bay Area.

Jessica Hische
Lettering artist

A lettering artist and author whose clients include Wes Anderson, American Express, Penguin Books, and The New York Times.

Lazy Bear
P.078

Shawn Raissi
Art director

A prolific art director with a taste for the good life. Brought up by the beaches of Orange County, now making waves in the San Francisco advertising scene.

Ken Ken
Ramen
P.081

Carlos Chavarría
Photographer

A photographer from Spain who fell in love with San Francisco and moved there from Madrid in 2010. Splits his time between shooting editorial work, personal projects, and eating chicken burritos.

Kristin Farr
Artist & journalist

An artist and journalist in San Francisco. Paints murals and smaller artworks, and interviews artists for Juxtapoz Magazine and KQED.

'aina
P.080

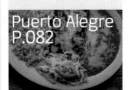

Puerto Alegre
P.082

Roman Muradov
Illustrator & author

An award-winning illustrator and the author of '(In A Sense) Lost & Found', 'Jacob Bladders and the State of the Art' and 'The End of A Fence'. Gold Medal winner from the Society of Illustrators.

Valencia
Pizza &
Pasta
P.084

Mike Davis
Owner, Everlasting Tattoo

Tattoo artist and owner of the world-renowned Everlasting Tattoo in San Francisco. An oil painter with works in prestigious private collections and museums worldwide.

Jackson Phillips
Musician

A musician under the name Day Wave.

Burma
Superstar
P.083

Homeroom
Mac &
Cheese
P.085

37 Four Barrel Coffee

Map B, P.104

Café hoppers will find Four Barrel Coffee the ultimate spot to perch, where the décor is social media-worthy, the crowd is interesting, and the coffee is widely acclaimed. Its beans are roasted in-house to retain their high quality, with most of them directly sourced from all around the world. Learn more about them by asking the baristas or checking online for a class you can attend, then pair your cuppa with a snack as you admire the local artwork on display. If you are still hungry afterwards, head to its sister outlet The Mill (#38) for a pizza dinner.

🕐 0700-2000 daily
🏠 375 Valencia St, CA 94103
📞 (415) 896 4289
URL fourbarrelcoffee.com

EDGES
ANNAMARIE PABST
SEAN CARPENTER
JUSTIN TOVIL
ALICE MARSHALL

"Get a pour-over coffee and chat with the barista to learn more about the coffee you're having."

– Kevin Tudball

📍 **38** **The Mill**
Map I, P.109

If you think coffee and bread make the perfect pair, The Mill brings the best of these daily staples together brilliantly. Set up as a collaboration between Four Barrel Coffee (#37) and Josey Baker Bread, classic pour-overs, aromatic espressos, fresh pastries and toasts topped with tasty things pretty much sum up a menu that locals cannot get enough of. Its bright and lofty home-kitchen-like set-up is welcoming, but many also enjoy takeaways at the nearby Mt. Alamo Park when the weather is kind. Too light a meal? Go for a weekly special sandwich or their daily pizza nights.

🕐 0700-2100 daily
🏠 736 Divisadero Street, CA 94117
📞 (415) 345 1953
URL www.themillsf.com

"Get coffee and toast."
– Casey Martin

39 Outerlands
Map J, P.109

With its weathered wooden walls, up-cycled furniture, mellow lighting, and easy rustic vibes, Outerlands may look just like any other hip urban eatery at first glance. However, tuck into the Dutch pancake or Eggs in Jail for brunch, and the reason it is one of the city's most exciting culinary destinations becomes apparent. Besides its ideal location just a few blocks away from the ocean, its kitchen prepares fresh and delicious local fare using sustainable resources at every opportunity. Settle in with the perfect balance of honest food and comfy beach-chic décor.

🕐 0900-1500, 1700-2200 daily
🏠 4001 Judah St, CA 94122
📞 (415) 661 6140
URL outerlandssf.com
🖉 Brunch available on Sa, Su only

"Go early and often. Sit outside, wrap up with a blanket, and watch the fog roll in."

– Jenny Gheith

40 Tartine Manufactory
Map B, P.104

Tartine Manufactory is a stellar example of a multi-hyphenate establishment – a restaurant, bar, ice creamery, bakery, and café – that is held together by expert craftsmanship. Set up as a platform of collaboration for the community after the success of its predecessor, Tartine Bakery, anything from its potentially overwhelming selection of bread and pastry offerings is not to be missed. The sky-high ceilings, light wooden finishes, and delicate paper lanterns in the space create a cosy dine-in atmosphere. Afterwards, drop by Heath Ceramics (#26) to pick up a gift or two.

🕐 0800–2200 daily
🏠 595 Alabama St, CA 94110
📞 (415) 757 0007
URL www.tartinemanufactory.com

"[It's great for] breakfast, lunch or dinner."
– Tung Chiang

41 20th Century Cafe
Map A, P.102

Housed in a building that was once owned by famed cartoonist R.L. 'Rube' Goldberg, 20th Century Cafe will transport you straight back to the 1900s with its music, tableware, and dreamy décor inspired by the owner's travels through Vienna, Prague, and Budapest. Its modest but mouthwatering menu celebrates Californian produce by drawing much inspiration from vintage cookbooks, movies, and food – backed by 20+ years of cooking and baking experience. Squeeze a little sunshine into your day by indulging in its sweet treats, particularly the Russian Honey Cake, in between meals.

🕐 0800–1730 (Mo–Fr), 1000–1730 (Sa), –1600 (Su)
🏠 198 Gough St, CA 94102
📞 (415) 621 2380
🔗 www.20thcenturycafe.com

"Go for afternoon tea!"

– Natalie So

42 Lazy Bear

Map B, P.104

What started as a local pop-up restaurant is now a Michelin-starred beacon for the San Francisco dining scene. Lazy Bear makes for the ideal modern dinner party venue without the stuffiness, especially if you are travelling in a big group. Delicious Northern American fare is served from an open kitchen straight onto giant communal tables to encourage curiosity and conversations between diners and chefs. With just one tasting menu and two seatings every night, it is an intimate experience that will change the way you enjoy dinner and drinks with strangers.

🕐 1800-2300 (Tu-Sa)
🏠 3416 19th St, CA 94110
📞 (415) 874 9921
URL www.lazybearsf.com
🔗 No phone reservations, via website only

"Plan ahead. Big time. There's usually mid-week availability a couple of weeks out for small parties, and weekends are fairly impossible."
– Jessica Hische

43 'aina
Map B, P.105

Hawaiian cuisine has slowly but surely found its footing in the mainstream culinary world in recent years, and deservedly so. However, 'aina takes it a step further by reinventing typical flavours into a titillating brunch menu, and elevating indigenous fare into an exquisite gastronomic experience come sundown. Using local and specially imported ingredients straight from the islands, the chefs truly capture sunshine on a plate. With its aloha spirit-infused hospitality and foliage-filled interior, this restaurant is the breath of fresh air and originality that you (and your palate) have been looking for.

🕐 1000-1430 (Fr), 0900- (Sa, Su), 1730-2200 (We-Su)
🏠 900 22nd St, CA 94107 📞 (415) 814 3815
🔗 www.ainasf.com 📎 Brunches for walk-ins only, dinner reservations via website

"The Kalbi Loco Moco is an awesome interpretation of a classic dish without the classic coma that traditionally comes after."
– Shawn Raissi

44 KEN KEN RAMEN
Map B, P.104

The quest to find delicious and filling ramen in any city is always challenging, but save yourself the trouble with Ken Ken Ramen. Whether you prefer more traditional broths like tonkotsu and miso, slightly more experimental ones, or vegetarian options, indulge in some authentic flavours while soaking in the restaurant's fun and vibrant energy. It only serves Japanese curry made from ramen broth in the afternoon, so plan your visit if you have noodle-based cravings to sate. Sneak a peek into the washroom before you leave.

🕐 1800–2200 (Tu–Su), 1200–1530 (Su) [Ramen];
1130–1500 (Mo–Sa) [Curry]
🏠 3378 18th St, CA 94117 📞 (415) 967 2636
URL kenkenramen.com 🖎 Deliveries available

"Get there with time; it can get really crowded!"
– Carlos Chavarría

45 Puerto Alegre
Map B, P.104

Given how seriously the locals take their burritos, it comes as no surprise that the city is peppered with delightful Mexican eateries that cater to varying personal tastes. Beyond its authentic fare, Puerto Alegre stands out for its cosy, unpretentious atmosphere and amazing margaritas that tend to go down a little too easily. A family business that has spanned generations since 1970, it dishes up heart-warming comfort food in old-fashioned combination plates with generous portions that are fun to share. Choose the outdoor seating area to feel the buzz from the street.

🕐 1000-2200 (Mo), 1700-2300 (Tu), 1100-2300 (We-Su) 🏠 546 Valencia St, CA 94110 📞 (415) 255 8201
URL www.puertoalegresf.net

"Go early! After 6pm, you may have a long wait. While you wait, explore nearby shops and bars across the street."
– Kristin Farr

46 Burma Superstar
Map D, P.107

Since its humble beginnings in 1992, Burma Superstar has played a huge part in popularising a cuisine that often still flies under the radar. Serving scrumptious flavours from Myanmar and its surrounding regions in generous-sized portions, regulars swear by its traditional menu items while the adventurous will be appeased by its updated classics, where the tealeaf salad and samusa soups are sure to hit the spot. Although it is slightly off the beaten path, visit during off-peak hours to avoid the huge lunch and dinner crowds.

🕐 1130-1500 (Mo-Su), 1700-2130 (Su-Th), -2200 (Fr, Sa)
🏠 309 Clement St, CA 94118
📞 (415) 387 2147
URL www.burmasuperstar.com

"If the line is too long, try Mandalay nearby! It may be just as good."

– Roman Muradov

47 Valencia Pizza & Pasta
Map B, P.104

San Francisco may be known as a food paradise, but most people hardly look beyond the surface. Amongst the award-winning restaurants, hipster eateries, novelty joints, and stuffy franchises, places like Valencia Pizza & Pasta offer relief with its fuss-free menu of classic Italian favourites done well. Regulars know that its low-key, dive-y atmosphere masks a wide range of delicious meals in huge portions at affordable prices. Start your day with a hearty breakfast, or fuel up after an afternoon of exploring the neighbourhood.

🕐 1100-1500 (Mo-Fr), 0900- (Sa, Su), 1700-2130 (Mo-Sa) 🏠 801 Valencia St, CA 94110 📞 (415) 642 1882

"I prefer hidden, hole-in-the-wall type places [like this]."

– Mike Davis

48 Homeroom Mac & Cheese
Map O, P.111

If a restaurant exclusively dedicated to the cheesy comfort food sounds like a dream come true, you have Homeroom Mac & Cheese owner Erin Wade to thank for bringing it to life. Take a trip back in time amidst its funky schoolhouse décor and tuck into a perennial favourite that you can upgrade with an extensive variety of ingredient combinations – including vegetables for the health-conscious. Finding it hard to decide what to have? Go for the sampling platter, and then wash everything down with an ice-cold beer or some wine.

🕐 1100–2200 (Tu-Su)
🏠 400 40th St, Oakland, CA 94609
📞 (510) 597 0400
URL homeroom510.com

"One of my favourite restaurants in Oakland, it never gets old for me. I usually go with the gluten-free Gilroy Garlic and an iced tea."

– Jackson Phillips

Nightlife

Clubbing, live performances, and themed outings

Fun means many different things in San Francisco. To complement its vibrant dining scene, the city offers plenty of leisurely pursuits after sunset for purveyors of unlimited possibilities, those who seek quiet conversations with crafted cocktails, and everyone else in between. Party people looking to wear their dancing shoes out will find a myriad of clubbing options like 1015 Folsom (#53), a labyrinth of old and new beats where you could discover a new favourite genre, or Make Out Room (#56) and DNA Lounge (www.dnalounge. com) for blasts from the past. Live music fans will be spoilt for choice with gig venues, from historic sites like The Fillmore (#55), a legendary platform that has helped to propel the careers of many hall-of-fame worthy bands, to more intimate spaces like Hotel Utah Saloon (#54) and The Chapel (www.thechapelsf.com) where up-and-coming indie acts grace the stage. For something different yet no less memorable, art and culture appreciators can head to the SFJAZZ Center (#51) or San Francisco Ballet (www.sfballet.org) to catch inspiring performances, while nature lovers can explore the California Academy of Sciences (#49) – a planetarium, aquarium and natural history museum all under one roof – with drinks after dark. If you just need a nightcap in a cosy spot away from noisy carousers, there are more than enough stylish low-key bars and speakeasy-type nooks to hole up in.

Theresa Lee
Founder, Future Glory Co.

Designer, maker, entrepreneur, and founder of Future Glory Co., a socially conscious bag company in San Francisco.

Mission Bowling Club
P.091

Joshua & Lauren Podoll
Founders, The Podolls

The Podolls is the eponymous line of relaxed, wearable, and effortlessly beautiful handcrafted clothing – rooted in sustainability, global stewardship, and a commitment to centuries-old techniques and craftsmanship.

Kristina Varaksina
Photographer

A fine art, fashion, and portrait photographer based in San Francisco. Her work is represented at the Themes + Projects Gallery and more.

California Academy of Sciences
P.090

SFJAZZ Center
P.092

Max Gunawan
Founder, Lumio

Entrepreneur, designer, and founder of Lumio, a design brand based in San Francisco. Passionate about designing beautiful and functional products that combine craftsmanship and technology to help simplify modern living.

1015 Folsom
P.094

Montrey Whittaker
Founder, EARMILK.COM

Runs the online music publication EARMILK. Moved to San Francisco for the love of music. Finds the Bay Area a cultural hotbed, not just for music, but for all forms of self expression.

Un–
Design studio

A San Francisco-based design studio specialising in creative direction for companies large and small. Works collaboratively to define brands by delivering effective visual languages across all applications and media.

Castro Theatre
P.093

Hotel Utah Saloon
P.095

Claudia de Almeida
Graphic designer

A Brazil-born graphic designer based primarily in San Francisco. Co-owner of a design studio called 'o Banquinho', which is Portuguese for 'The Tiny Bank'.

Make Out Room
P.097

Pakayla Rae Biehn
Painter & set stylist

A painter and set stylist who lives and works in San Francisco.

ROGUE WAVE
Musicians

A rock band from Oakland that draws inspiration from the inevitable delusions of everyday American life.

The Fillmore
P.096

Tosca Cafe
P.098

Brady Patrick Boyle
Graphic designer

A graphic designer living and working in the Mission district, with a focus on branding and identity. Enjoys creating the problem as well as the tools with which to solve it.

Benjamin Cooper
P.100

Apexer
Artist

A San Francisco-born street artist who creates colourful, abstract patterns through the use of spray paint. His work has been shown extensively, both in the Bay Area and abroad.

Corey Lee
Restaurant owner & chef

Moved to San Francisco in 2009 and opened his first restaurant, Benu, followed by a French-inspired bistro called Monsieur Benjamin, and a collaborative restaurant project at SFMOMA called In Situ.

St. Mary's Club
P.099

Lone Palm
P.101

49 California Academy Of Sciences

Map H, P.109

If you happen to be in or around Golden Gate Park on a Thursday, drop by the California Academy of Sciences after sundown when it transforms into an enchanting space for explorers over 21 years of age. Visitors are allowed after-hours access to all exhibits for a themed journey each week, taking them to outer space, the pre-historic world, or through the depths of the sea. With special pro-grammes, live music, and cocktails involved, it is a unique way to visit the planetarium, aquarium, and natural history museum that are all under one living roof.

🕒 *1800-2100 (Th)* 💲 *$22/$15* 🏠 *55 Music Concourse Dr, CA 94118* 📞 *(415) 379 8000* 🔗 *www.calacademy.org/nightlife* 🖉 *For 21+ with ID*

"*Come a little earlier and visit the de Young museum which is the building next door.*"

– Theresa Lee

50 Mission Bowling Club
Map B, P.104

While it offers a fun night out doing what its name suggests, the Mission Bowling Club is also an award-winning culinary destination where local hipsters hang out. Its kitchen churns out comfort food that defies expectations with locally sourced, seasonal ingredients, while the stylish bar serves specialty cocktails along with a rotating craft beer and wine list. The creative starters and juicy burgers go perfectly with an ice-cold beverage or two. Be sure to ask for a table at the mezzanine-level seating area, where you can have a bird's-eye view of the lanes as you grab your bite.

🕐 1500-2300 (Mo-We), -0000 (Th, Fr), 1100-0000 (Sa), -2300 (Su)
💲 Lanes from $38/hour 🏠 3176 17th St, CA 94110 📞 (415) 863 2695
🔗 missionbowlingclub.com
🔗 For 21+; families welcomed 1100-1900 (Sa, Su) only

"Reserve a table and a lane in advance because spaces fill up quickly!"

– Joshua & Lauren Podoll

51 SFJAZZ Center
Map A, P.102

Hailed as one of the greatest jazz halls in the world, the SFJAZZ Center is the first stand-alone structure in the country that was built specifically for its genre and other related forms of music. With an annual festival, summer sessions, and up to 300 varied live performances a year as mainstay programmes, it is a cultural institution that celebrates the spirited local scene and its aspiring talents through pristine acoustics and thoughtfully designed spaces. Check online for showtimes or workshop and class schedules to learn more about this fluid art form.

 ⏰ 1100–1730/end of final show (Tu-Sa); 90mins before shows (Su, Mo) [Box Office] 🏠 201 Franklin St, CA 94102 📞 (866) 920 5299
URL www.sfjazz.org

"Even though San Francisco is a very relaxed city in general, SFJAZZ is a place where you should dress nicely."
– Kristina Varaksina

52 Castro Theatre
📍 Map B, P.104

An iconic building in the heart of a neighbourhood symbolic all around the world for LGBT activism, the Castro Theatre is more than just a historic landmark with a cinematic façade. One of the country's few still-functioning movie palaces from the 1920s, it continues to entertain audiences with a fantastic line-up of musicals, plays, events, sketches, and more. The ornate décor and elegant set-up may reek of nostalgia for some, but the state-of-the-art sound system will boom you back into the present. Check its calendar online to plan your visit around a show.

🕐 Box office opens 30mins before 1st screening 💲 Entry fees vary with events 🏠 429 Castro St, CA 94114 📞 (415) 621 6120 🔗 www.castrotheatre.com

"Try to get a seat on the first row balcony. Sneak up there if you have to. You'll get the best vantage point (of both the interior and the movie screen)."

– Max Gunawan

53 1015 Folsom
Map A, P.102

Even if you are not up for partying until dawn, the 20,000-sq ft dance mecca that is 1015 Folsom is worth a peek. With five separate areas spread out over three floors, it has played host to an incredible number of acts, and continues to pull in the masses with a broad range of genre-based nights spanning from EDM to Latin. While the interiors may exude swanky undertones or hints of grandiosity depending on the area (like the 400-sq ft water wall video display), it is the understated building exterior that reflects the actual spirit of the club - which is all about the music.

🕐 2200-0200 (Th, Fr)
💲 Entry fees vary with events   📞 (415) 991 1015
🏠 1015 Folsom St, CA 94103   URL 1015.com
🔗 For 21+ with ID; tickets available via website

"This is a place you should go for the music itself, more so than anything else."

– Montrey Whittaker

54 Hotel Utah Saloon
Map A, P.103

The most intriguing venues often come with a sketchy past, and the Hotel Utah Saloon has amassed plenty of stories since 1908 – having been frequented by everybody from politicians and gamblers to fancy miscreants with a taste for danger. Today, it is a San Francisco institution featuring nightly live music by local and touring bands, as well as one of the best open mic sessions in town. With its intimate setting, state-of-the-art sound, freshly made menu and full bar, expect a great night out.

🕐 1130-0200 daily [Kitchen: -2300]
🏠 500 4th St, CA 94107
📞 (415) 546 6300
URL www.hotelutah.com

"It's a perfect place to meet up with friends and listen to a band or two and then head over to the bar, or the other way around."

– Un-

55 **The Fillmore**
Map E, P.107

Originally designed to be an Italianate-style
dance hall, The Fillmore has been a revered
institution in the San Francisco music scene
since the 1910s. Its hallowed stages have hosted
and launched the careers of noteworthy bands
and performers over the years, reaching its
height of popularity when it had a hand in
nudging hippie culture into mainstream coun-
ter-culture status. While it has gone through
many owners, the venue continues to attract
amazing artists and fans from all over the
world with the electric atmosphere that the
space creates. Check online for the latest information on the bands playing.

🕐 **S** *Hours & entry fees vary with events*
🏠 *805 Geary Blvd, CA 94115*
📞 *(415) 346-3000*
URL *thefillmore.com*

"*A great and iconic SF music venue.*"
– Claudia de Almeida

56 Make Out Room
Map B, P.104

Take a break from fancy and flashy clubs by getting your groove on at the Make Out Room. While its playlist covers classic genres like funk, reggae, and hip hop, its unique décor is committed to nostalgia with a shiny disco ball, hanging tinsel, and stage drapes – shimmying you back to the good ol' times. Indie music dominates happy hours, while live DJ and vinyl gigs make for fun nights out. Be warned: Slow Jams on Tuesday evenings, dedicated to the slower side of soul, might unwittingly result in prom night flashbacks in all its awkward glory.

🕐 1800-0200 daily
🏠 3225 22nd St, CA 94110
📞 (415) 647 2888
🌐 www.makeoutroom.com
🏷 For 21+ with ID

"Bar is cash only! Tip your bartenders well, they work hard and it's Tuesday."

– Pakayla Rae Biehn

57 Tosca Cafe
Map G, P.108

With its dim lighting, red leather chairs, chequered floors, and smoke-stained murals, the rehabilitated local landmark that is Tosca Cafe cocoons you with its warm, speakeasy vibes from the moment you enter. While it currently serves classic Italian dishes with a refreshing contemporary twist, echoes of the past remain in this once-notorious dive bar that saw countless legendary nights instigated by the city's eccentric and creative set. Drop by for a drink or two even if you are not up for a meal.

🕐 1700-0200 [Bar], 1800-0100 [Dining]
🏠 242 Columbus Ave, CA 94133
📞 (415) 986 9651
🌐 toscacafesf.com
🖉 Phone & online reservations for up to 6 pax

"Tosca has such a great sense of North Beach history. Old-school cocktails with fine food. Head to Vesuvio for a nightcap after!"
– Rogue Wave

58 St. Mary's Pub
Map L, P.110

Nurse your hangover with the hair of the dog at St. Mary's Pub, a one-of-its-kind neighbourhood bar in the Mission district that specialises in different incarnations of the Bloody Mary. If you were never a fan of the cocktail, this place might change your mind – whether you drink it classically styled or with a quirky cultural twist. Locals flock here to watch their favourite sports, play some pinball and pool, or simply chill out with cheap drinks to an eclectic but crowd-pleasing playlist.

🕐 1600–0200 (Mo–Fr), 1200– (Sa, Su)
🏠 3845 Mission St, CA 94110
📞 (415) 529 1325
🔗 stmaryspub.com

"Keep an eye out for punk rock legends. Fat Wreck Chords shop/studio is around the corner and those dudes are in there all the time."

– Brady Patrick Boyle

 **59 Benjamin Cooper**
Map A, P.102

Bars without signage can often provide some of the most memorable experiences, as Benjamin Cooper can confirm. There are two ways to find it – via the unmarked white door along Mason St, or the Hotel G lobby. Supposedly named after a local anti-Prohibition hero who dedicated his life to fine spirits (or so the owners want you to believe), it is an unpretentious hidden gem that boasts innovatively crafted cocktails, an intimate ambience, fun tunes, and friendly staff. Pair your drinks with some fresh oysters for a classic night out in a city known for its amazing seafood.

🕐 1700-0200 (Mo-Fr), 1800-0200 (Sa)
🏠 398 Geary St, CA 94102
📞 (415) 654 5061
🔗 benjamincoopersf.com

 "The atmosphere is perfect to enjoy a great drink in or to meet someone new."
– Apexer

60 Lone Palm
Map B, P.104

Understated and cool without trying too hard,
Lone Palm's laidback ambiguity is what makes
it a charming watering hole above the rest in
the Mission district. While its décor seems to
pay homage to a Miami cocktail bar from the
1950s with an abundance of neon, tea light
candles on white tablecloths, and hints of palm
trees, its drinks selection is pretty decent with
refillable small plates of free snacks to accom-
pany your tipple of choice. Get drunk on cosy
conversations until the wee hours.

🕐 1600–0200 (daily)
🏠 3394 22nd St, CA 94110
📞 (415) 648 0109

*"Casual but not too dive-y, the atmosphere is great
for an intimate gathering."*
– Corey Lee

- 8_Cathedral Of Saint Mary Of The Assumption
- 11_ 140 Maiden Lane
- 12_ Contemporary Jewish Museum
- 16_Spoke Art
- 30_Ver Unica
- 41_20th Century Cafe
- 51_SFJAZZ Center
- 53_1015 Folsom
- 59_Benjamin Cooper

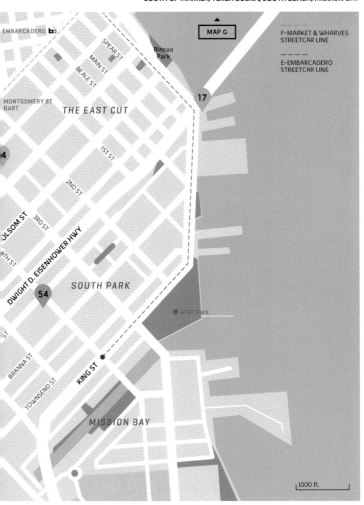

MAP G

F-MARKET & WHARVES
STREETCAR LINE

E-EMBARCADERO
STREETCAR LINE

1000 ft.

- 14_SFMOMA
- 17_Pier 24 Photography
- 54_Hotel Utah Saloon

- 10_Mission Dolores Park
- 18_Minnesota Street Project
- 20_826 Valencia / Pirate Supply Shop
- 21_Clarion Alley
- 22_StoreFrontLab
- 23_500 Capp Street
- 26_Heath Ceramics
- 28_The Aesthetic Union
- 29_Gravel & Gold
- 34_Paxton Gate
- 36_Bi-Rite Market

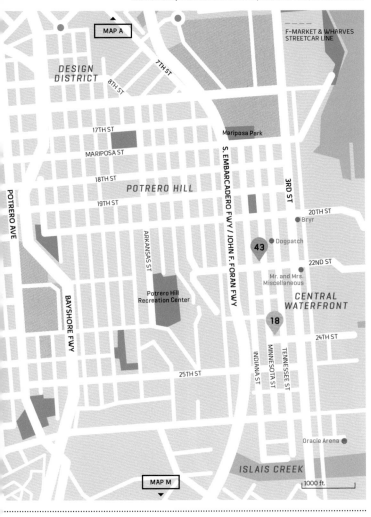

- 37_Four Barrel Coffee
- 40_Tartine Manufactory
- 42_Lazy Bear
- 43_'aina
- 44_Ken Ken Ramen
- 45_Puerto Alegre
- 47_Valencia Pizza & Pasta
- 50_Mission Bowling Club
- 52_Castro Theatre
- 56_Make Out Room
- 60_Lone Palm

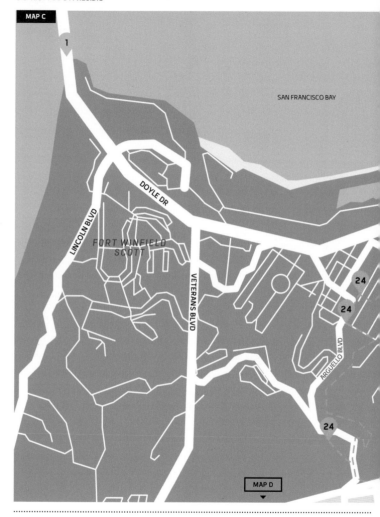

MAP C

SAN FRANCISCO BAY

1

DOYLE DR

LINCOLN BLVD

FORT WINFIELD SCOTT

VETERANS BLVD

ARGUELLO BLVD

24

24

24

MAP D
▼

- 1_Golden Gate Bridge
- 24_Goldsworthy in the
  Presidio

- 7_Palace of Fine Arts
- 24_Goldsworthy in the Presidio
- 25_Song Tea
- 27_Park Life
- 46_Burma Superstar
- 55_The Fillmore

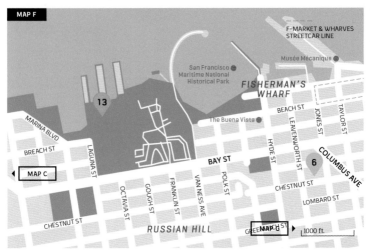

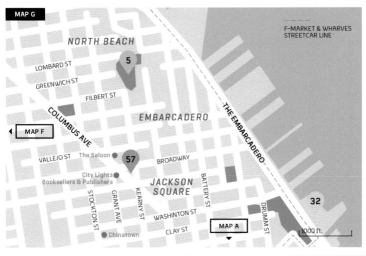

- 5_Coit Tower
- 6_San Francisco Art Institute
- 13_Fort Mason Center for Arts & Culture
- 32_Ferry Building Marketplace
- 57_Tosca Cafe

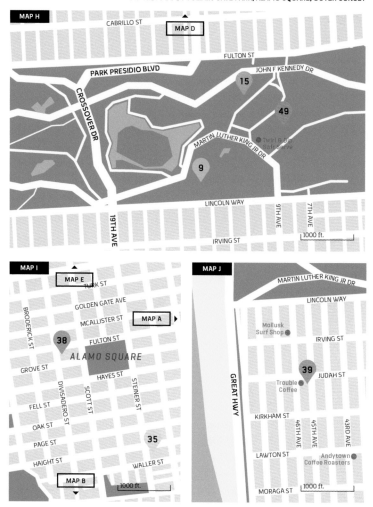

- 9_San Francisco Botanical Garden
- 15_de Young Museum
- 35_Vinyl Dreams
- 38_The Mill
- 39_Outerlands
- 49_California Academy of Sciences

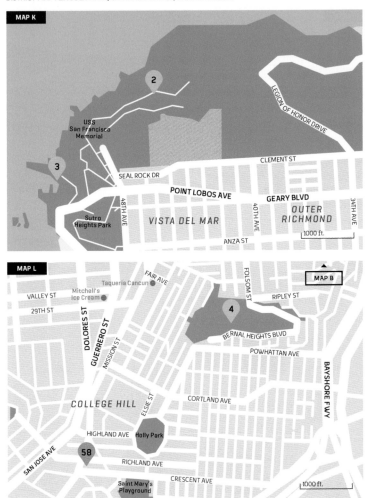

- 2_Lands End
- 3_Sutro Baths
- 4_Bernal Heights Hill
- 58_St. Mary's Pub

MAP M

S. EMBARCADERO FWY
EVANS AVE
MAP B
PHELPS ST
JERROLD ST
HUDSON AVE
33
INNES AVE
NEWHALL ST
3RD ST
OAKDALE AVE
PALOU AVE

1000 ft.

MAP N

27TH ST
26TH ST
25TH ST
JOHN B. WILLIAMS FWY
NORTHGATE AVE
Firebrand Artisan Breads
Humphry Slocombe
19
GRAND AVE
23TH ST
VALDEZ ST
TELEGRAPH AVE
BROADWAY
UPTOWN
THOMAS L BERKLEY WAY
19TH ST/ OAKLAND
19TH ST
17TH ST
Oaklandish
15TH ST

1000 ft.

MAP O

TEMESCAL
42ND ST
48
BROADWAY
GILBERT ST
41ST ST
40TH ST
WEBSTER ST
SHAFTER AVE
MANILA AVE
PIEDMONT AVENUE
HOWE ST
PIEDMONT AVE
Issues
W MACARTHUR BLVD

1000 ft.

MAP P

HASTE ST
Amoeba Music
People's Park
DWIGHT WAY
DANA ST
TELEGRAPH AVE
Willard Park
BENVENE AVE
COLLEGE AVE
STUART ST
RUSSELL ST
31
ASHBY AVE

1000 ft.

· ·

- 19_Creative Growth
- 31_Tail of the Yak
- 33_Flora Grubb Gardens
- 48_Homeroom Mac & Cheese

Accommodation

Hip hostels, fully-equipped apartments & swanky hotels

No journey is perfect without a good night's sleep to recharge. Whether you are on vacation or a business trip, our picks combine top quality and convenience, whatever your budget.

 < $100    $101–250 $251+

Inn at the Presidio

Bask in the beauty of the Presidio forest at this elegant modern inn that oozes with old-world charm. Located within walking distance of hiking trails and historical sites, it is the perfect cocoon from which to seek out authentic San Francisco adventures, with complimentary wine and cheese receptions in the evenings.

 42 Moraga Ave (Presidio of SF), CA 94129
(415) 800 7356
 www.presidiolodging.com/inn-at-the-presidio

Palace Hotel

Indulge in a luxurious stay at this local icon, where contemporary plush comforts and stylish designer décor blend seamlessly with exquisite classical touches. As the largest premier hotel in the world when it was first established in 1875, it continues to offer an opulent experience that reflects its rich heritage.

🏠 2 New Montgomery St, CA 94105
📞 (415) 512 1111
URL www.sfpalace.com

The Battery

🏠 717 Battery St, CA 94111
📞 (415) 230 8000
🔗 www.thebatterysf.com

Proper Hotel

🏠 1100 Market St, CA 94102
📞 (415) 735 7777
🔗 www.properhotel.com/hotels/san-francisco

Hotel Spero

🏠 405 Taylor St, CA 94102
📞 (415) 885 2500
🌐 www.hotelspero.com

Hotel G

🏠 386 Geary St, CA 94102
📞 (415) 986 2000
🌐 www.hotelgsanfrancisco.com

Music City Hotel

🏠 1353 Bush St, CA 94109
📞 (415) 816 6207
🌐 musiccityhotel.org

Notes

Index

Photography

Carlos Chavarría, *p081*
www.carloschavarria.com

Greg Lutze, *p034*
vsco.co

June Kim, *p037*
www.june-kim.com

Kristina Varaksina, *p092*
kristinavaraksina.com

Publishing

Jameson Alexander, *p040*
www.parklifestore.com

Montrey Whittaker, *p094*
earmilk.com

Natalie So, *p077*
www.natalie.so

Photo & other credits

1015 FOLSOM, *p088 & p094*
(p088, p094 top & middle) 1015
FOLSOM, Demian Becerra

Bernal Heights Hill, *p017*
(All) Bernal Heights Hill, San
Francisco Recreation and Park
Department

Bi-Rite Market, *p067*
(All) Bi-Rite Market

**California Academy of
Sciences,** *p086 & p090*
(All) California Academy of
Sciences *(p090 bottom)* Kathryn
Whitney

Castro Theatre, *p093*
(Top) Helder Ribeiro / CC BY-SA 2.0

**Cathedral of Saint Mary of the
Assumption,** *p021*
(All) Cathedral of Saint Mary of
the Assumption *(Top)* Catholic San
Francisco/Deb Greenblatt *(Bottom)*
ADSF/Eugene Caputo

Coit Tower, *p018*
(All) COIT TOWER, San Francisco
Recreation and Park Department

**Contemporary Jewish
Museum,** *p025*
(All) Contemporary Jewish
Museum *(Top)* Yerba Buena Lane
(Middle right & bottom left) Mark

Darley *(Bottom right)* Gary Sexton
Photography

Creative Growth, *p040*
(All) Creative Growth, Diana
Rothery *(Middle)* Lulu Sotelo and
Lynn Pisco *(Bottom)* Allan Lofberg

de Young Museum, *p034–035*
(All) California Academy of
Sciences, Fine Arts Museums
of San Francisco *(p034 top)* de
Young Museum in Golden Gate
Park *(Middle)* Overlook *(Bottom)*
Osher Sculpture Garden *(p035
top)* Oceanic Arts Gallery *(Middle
left)* American Gallery *(Middle
right)* "California Spring" by Albert
Bierstadt *(Bottom)* Contemporary
Gallery

Ferry Building Marketplace,
p062–063
(p062 top, p063 middle & top right)
Ferry Building Marketplace, Nat
& Cody

Flora Grubb Gardens, *p064*
(All) Flora Grubb Gardens, Caitlin
Atkinson

**Fort Mason Center for Arts &
Culture,** *p030*
(Middle & bottom) Fort Mason
Center for Arts & Culture *(Middle)*
Sophie Calle: Take Care of
Yourself *(Bottom)* Robert Campbell
Photography

Four Barrel Coffee, *p068 &
p072–073*
(All) Four Barrel Coffee *(All except
p073 bottom)* Eric Wolfinger *(p073
bottom)* Kevin Ellison

Goldsworthy in the Presidio,
p047
(Bottom) Jay Graham

Heath Ceramics, *p048 &
p054–055*
(All) Heath Ceramics *(All except red
canopy)* Mariko Reed

Lazy Bear, *p078–079*
(All) Lazy Bear *(p078 top)* Finch
Photography *(p079)* Kassie
Borreson

Mission Bowling Club, *p088
& p091*
(Top) Mission Bowling Club

Mission Dolores Park, *p023*
(All) MISSION DOLORES PARK, San

Francisco Recreation and Park
Department

Palace of Fine Arts, *p010 & p020*
(All) Palace of Fine Arts, Non Plus
Ultra

Paxton Gate, *p065*
(All) Paxton Gate *(Top &
bottom)* Saenz *(Middle)* Tev Lee
Photography

San Francisco Art Institute,
p019
(All) San Francisco Art Institute
(Bottom) Diego Rivera, The Making
of a Fresco Showing the Building of
a City, 1931, Fresco, 271 by 357 inches,
Gift of William Gerstle

**San Francisco Botanical
Garden,** *p022*
(All) San Francisco Botanical
Garden *(Top & middle)* Saxon Holt
(Bottom) Travis Lange

SFJAZZ Center, *p092*
(All) SFJAZZ *(Top)* Henrik Kam
(Middle) Jay Blakesberg *(Bottom)*
Drew Altizer

SFMOMA, *p026 & p031–033*
(All) SFMOMA *(p026, p031 top &
bottom, p032–033)* Henrik Kam
(p031 middle) Jon McNeal, Snøhetta

StoreFrontLab, *p044–045*
(All) StoreFrontLab

Tartine Manufactory, *p076*
(All) Tartine Manufactory

The Fillmore, *p096*
(Middle) The Poster Room by
Dianne Yee / CC BY-ND 2.0 *(Bottom)*
BRMC @ The Fillmore San
Francisco 4/22/13 by swimfinfan /
CC BY-SA 2.0

The Golden Gate Bridge, *p014*
(All) From the holdings of the
Golden Gate Bridge, Highway and
Transportation District

Tosca Cafe, *p098*
(All) Tosca Cafe

–

In Accommodation: all courtesy of
respective hotels

The Battery, *p114*
(All) The Battery, Douglas
Friedman

CITIX60

CITIx60: San Francisco

Published and distributed by
viction workshop ltd

viction:ary™

7C Seabright Plaza, 9-23 Shell Street,
North Point, Hong Kong

Url: www.victionary.com
Email: we@victionary.com
🅕 @victionworkshop
🐦 @victionary_
📷 @victionworkshop

Edited and produced by viction:ary

Concept & art direction: Victor Cheung
Research & editorial: YuetLin Lim
Project Coordination: Katherine Wong, Leanne Lee
Design & map illustration: MW Wong, Raphael Kwok
Cover map illustration: Andrea Nguyen
Count to 10 illustrations: Guillaume Kashima aka Funny Fun
Photography: Jenny Diaz

© 2018 viction workshop ltd

All rights reserved. No part of this publication may be reproduced, stored in
retrieval systems or transmitted in any form or by any means, electronic,
mechanical, photocopying, recording or any information storage, without
written permissions of viction:ary.

Content is compiled based on facts available as of July 2018. Travellers are
advised to check for updates from respective locations before your visit.

First edition – August 2018
ISBN 978-988-78500-3-8
Printed and bound in China

Acknowledgements

A special thank you to all the creatives, photographers, editors, produc-
ers, companies, and organisations involved for your crucial contribu-
tions to our inspiration and knowledge necessary for the creation of
this book. And, to the many whose names are not credited but have
participated in the completion of this book, we thank you for your input
and continuous support.

CITIX60
City Guides

CITIx60 is a handpicked list of hotspots that illustrates the spirit of the world's most exhilarating design hubs. From what you see to where you stay, this city guide series leads you to experience the best — the places that only passionate insiders know and go.

Each volume is a unique collaboration with local creatives from selected cities. Known for their accomplishments in fields as varied as advertising, architecture, graphics, fashion, food, music as well as publishing, these locals are at the cutting edge of what's on and when. Whether it's a one-day stopover or a longer trip, **CITIx60** is your inspirational guide.

Stay tuned for new editions.

City guides available now:

Amsterdam	Portland
Barcelona	Singapore
Berlin	Stockholm
Copenhagen	Taipei
Hong Kong	Tokyo
Istanbul	Vancouver
Lisbon	Vienna
London	San Francisco
Los Angeles	
Melbourne	
Milan	
New York	
Paris	